ANONYMOUS

Abyss

"In the end, the scars remind us where we've been, but the fire in our veins tells us where we're going."

Anonymous

Contents

Foreword

This book is born from the chaos, the noise, and the silence in between. It's the voice you've buried, the rage you've tamed, and the fear you've learned to face. We live in a world that pushes you down, tells you to be quiet, but this is about breaking that mold. It's about screaming into the void and making sure the world hears it. These stories are for the ones who've fought, fallen, and got back up, ready to take on the next battle. If you're holding this, you're already halfway there. Let's go.

Acknowledgments

Special thanks to Eddson Lens from Pexels for the powerful photo used on the cover. Your work captured the raw energy and emotion that set the tone for this entire project. The image speaks louder than words, and we couldn't have asked for a better visual to represent what this book stands for.

Splintered Walls

I built these walls so high, thought they'd never fall,
  Thick as steel, so strong, I could take it all.
  But now they're splintered, every crack's a reminder,
  Of the weight I'm carryin', man, I'm feelin' it tighter.

Thought I was bulletproof, shut the world out,
  Didn't need nobody, didn't need the doubt.
  But these voices inside keep poundin' like fists,
  Every word, every hit, I'm losin' my grip.

I put up the bricks just to keep me from breakin',
  Now they're shakin', achin', all the pain I'm takin'.
  Told myself I'd never let 'em see the cracks,
  But these splinters are sharp, stabbin' in my back.

They told me, "Stay strong, just keep it together,"
  But I'm crumblin' slow, yeah, it feels like forever.
  The walls I built were meant to save me from fallin',
  Now they're caving in, man, the ground is callin'.

Every crack I see is a fear I can't hide,
  A battle in my mind that I fight every night.

Splintered walls show the weakness underneath,
And the truth cuts deep, like I'm losin' my feet.

Tried to hold it all in, like it didn't hurt,
Now the cracks in my armor are showin' my worth.
Splintered walls crumble, piece by piece,
And I'm stuck in this mess, searchin' for release.

Tired of pretendin', tired of the lie,
These splintered walls tell the truth, I can't deny.
But maybe when they fall, I'll finally see clear,
That the walls I built weren't keepin' out fear.

The Place I Can't Find

I'm lookin' for a place, man, somewhere to belong,
But every road I take just feels so wrong.
I'm stuck in the cracks, lost in the seams,
Chasin' a place that only lives in my dreams.

Everywhere I go, it's like I don't fit,
Like I'm standin' on the edge, about to quit.
I see their smiles, but it's all fake,
While inside, I'm drownin', more than I can take.

I'm searchin' for a home that I never knew,
Where the walls don't close in, where I'm not see-through.
But it's always just outta reach, slippin' fast,
The place I can't find is buried in the past.

I feel the pressure, feel it tight on my chest,
Like a weight I can't shake, I can't get no rest.
I'm screamin' inside but it don't make a sound,
Tryin' to find solid ground but I'm always knocked down.

I walk through the crowd but still feel alone,
Surrounded by faces, still, I'm on my own.

I need a place where I can breathe, feel alive,
But every turn I take, I'm just tryin' to survive.

Where's the place that makes sense of the mess in my mind?
I've been searchin', runnin', but it's nothin' I find.
They tell me, "Just hold on, you'll get there in time,"
But I'm stuck in a loop, repeatin' the climb.

No map to show me where I need to go,
No sign that says it's safe to let it show.
The place I can't find is the place I need,
But it's slippin' away, like a forgotten dream.

Maybe one day, I'll break out, break through,
Find a place that's real, where I can start new.
But right now, I'm lost, caught in the grind,
Still searchin' for the place I can't find.

Chasing Shadows

I'm runnin' fast, but it's right on my heels,
  The past creepin' in, man, this shit feels real.
  Every step I take, it's there in the dark,
  Like a ghost I can't shake, leavin' its mark.

Tried to bury it deep, keep it locked away,
  But no matter how far, it's never gone, it stays.
  I'm chasin' shadows, can't escape the fight,
  They're hauntin' my days, lurkin' through the night.

I thought if I ran fast enough, I'd leave it behind,
  But the memories stick, playin' tricks on my mind.
  Like a chain I can't break, it's draggin' me down,
  In the middle of nowhere, but I'm never found.

I'm chasin' shadows, fightin' to stay ahead,
  But every turn I make, I'm facin' what I dread.
  It's like I'm stuck in a loop, the past on repeat,
  No matter how far, I can't find my feet.

They say time heals, but I ain't seen proof,
  The shadows just grow, like I'm stuck in the truth.

I try to forget, push it out of sight,
But it's pullin' me back, never lettin' me fight.

It's in the silence, the noise in my head,
The echoes of words, the things I never said.
I'm runnin' from it all, but it's catchin' up fast,
The shadows of my past, man, they never pass.

I thought I'd outrun it, thought I'd be free,
But the shadows are part of the person I see.
I'm chasin' 'em down, but they're always there,
Remindin' me of pain that's too much to bear.

No matter where I go, no matter the pace,
The shadows are with me, they're stuck in the chase.
I can't shake 'em off, can't make 'em fade,
I'm runnin' from the past, but it's a game I've played.

Maybe one day, I'll stop, turn around,
Face the shadows that keep me underground.
But for now, I'm runnin', tryin' to stay ahead,
Chasin' shadows, livin' in the dread.

Beneath the Weight

I'm underneath it all, can't catch a breath,
    Feelin' the pressure like it's pushin' me to death.
    Expectations heavy, they're stackin' up high,
    I'm crackin' under it, but I gotta get by.

They say, "Be stronger, don't let it show,"
    But inside, I'm fallin', and they'll never know.
    Gotta wear the mask, like I'm holdin' my place,
    But beneath the weight, I'm losin' the race.

Every demand's a chain, tight around my throat,
    They tell me "fly," but I can barely float.
    Climbin' the ladder but the rungs keep breakin',
    Dreams I had, now they're there for the takin'.

But I can't reach 'em, they're slippin' away,
    Crushed by the voices, by what they say.
    "You're not enough, better get in line,"
    Feelin' the pressure, but pretendin' I'm fine.

It's a war I can't win, but they keep on fightin',
    Like the sun don't rise without them decidin'.

I'm beneath the weight, can't see the light,
Stuck in this battle, losin' the fight.

They pile it on, like I ain't breakin',
But inside, I'm shakin', feelin' like I'm fakin'.
Tellin' me, "Man up, you better not fall,"
But I'm drownin' beneath the weight of it all.

The higher I go, the harder it gets,
Crushed by the burden, the fear and regrets.
They want perfection, but I'm just a kid,
Tryin' to carry it all, but my strength's runnin' thin.

I'm screamin' inside but it don't make a sound,
The world keeps spinnin', I'm stuck to the ground.
Beneath the weight, I'm breakin' apart,
Holdin' it together, but it's killin' my heart.

I wanna be free, wanna let go,
But the pressure's a wave, and I'm caught in the flow.
Beneath the weight, I'm losin' my fight,
Just tryin' to make it, to get through the night.

Maybe one day, I'll rise from the strain,
But for now, I'm drownin' in this endless pain.
Beneath the weight, it's crushin' me still,
And I'm trapped in the silence, against my will.

Echoes of Silence

I hear the silence, but it's screamin' in my head,
   Like a thousand voices, wishin' I was dead.
   The noise cuts deep, but there's nothin' to say,
   I'm drownin' in the quiet, can't push it away.

Thought I'd find peace, thought I'd find calm,
   But the silence hits harder, like a ticking bomb.
   The walls are closin' in, can't take the space,
   Echoes of silence, I can't escape this place.

It's in the emptiness, it's in the void,
   Every word I don't say, I'm feelin' destroyed.
   Tried to speak up, but my voice went still,
   Now I'm lost in the quiet, can't feel the thrill.

Every second's heavy, every minute's slow,
   Echoes of silence are all I know.
   I built this cage, and now I'm stuck inside,
   Feelin' the weight of everything I hide.

The air's too thick, I can't seem to breathe,
   The silence wraps tight, it'll never leave.

No one hears the war goin' on in my mind,
I'm trapped in the quiet, lost in the grind.

I scream, but the sound just dies in the air,
Like nobody's listenin', like nobody's there.
I'm fallin' apart, but I keep it contained,
Echoes of silence, the scars still remain.

They say silence is golden, but it feels like a curse,
Like I'm stuck in reverse, everything gets worse.
It's a deafening roar, but it's all in my brain,
Echoes of silence are drivin' me insane.

I thought I'd be free when the noise went away,
But now I'm just left with nothin' to say.
The quiet's a prison, I'm trapped in the void,
In this echo of silence, I'm self-destroyed.

Maybe one day, I'll break through the still,
But right now, it's heavy, can't feel the thrill.
Echoes of silence, they're here to stay,
And I'm lost in the quiet, just wastin' away.

Running in Place

I've been runnin' for miles, but I'm still stuck here,
  Chasin' my demons, drownin' in fear.
  Thought I'd break free, thought I'd escape,
  But the same damn problems keep changin' their shape.

It's like I'm movin', but nothin' gets clear,
  No matter how fast, the end's never near.
  I'm fightin' the current, trapped in the race,
  Feelin' like I'm stuck, just runnin' in place.

Every time I break, I rebuild again,
  But the cracks keep showin' through this broken skin.
  I try to run faster, but the weight won't shift,
  Carryin' the past like a curse I can't lift.

They tell me, "Keep pushin', you'll get out someday,"
  But I'm circlin' back, stuck on replay.
  Like I'm runnin' on ice, can't get no traction,
  Just sinkin' deeper in my own reaction.

I'm runnin' in place, I'm caught in the grind,
  Chasin' my tail, losin' my mind.

It's a loop I can't break, no matter the pace,
Every step I take, I'm runnin' in place.

I thought I was leavin' it all behind,
But the past comes back, like it's stitched to my mind.
I can't outrun it, can't make it fade,
The harder I push, the more it's delayed.

I'm screamin' inside but the world don't hear,
I'm drownin' in doubt, suffocatin' in fear.
I reach for the edge but it's always too far,
Like I'm chasin' a light that don't leave a scar.

Every plan I make falls apart in my hands,
Like buildin' castles outta dust and sand.
I'm runnin' in circles, burnin' in place,
Feelin' like I'm stuck in an endless space.

They say, "Keep goin', you'll find your way,"
But every step I take just leads me to stay.
I'm runnin' from nothin', fightin' the strain,
But I'm trapped in the storm, drownin' in rain.

Maybe one day I'll break the chain,
But for now, I'm stuck, trapped in the pain.
Runnin' in place, like I'll never break free,
Caught in the cycle that's swallowin' me.

Burn the Bridges

I lit the match, watched the flames grow high,
  Sick of the lies, now it's time to say goodbye.
  Burnin' the bridges, I don't need the weight,
  But the ashes fall heavy, like it's too late.

They told me who to be, told me how to act,
  But now I'm takin' my life back, that's a fact.
  Cut the ropes, break the ties, I'm settin' it ablaze,
  But the fear creeps in, in a smoke-filled haze.

I can feel the heat, but the cold's still there,
  Cut myself loose, now I'm gaspin' for air.
  It's hard to walk away when the flames burn bright,
  But I'm sick of the darkness, searchin' for the light.

I burn the bridges, leave it all behind,
  But in the wreckage, it's myself I find.
  The fear of isolation, it's pullin' me near,
  But I'd rather be alone than livin' in fear.

They say, "You'll regret it, you'll come crawlin' back,"
  But I'm done with the pressure, tired of the act.

I burned the bridges, can't go back now,
But the emptiness follows, like a shadow somehow.

The flames rise higher, but so does the pain,
Like I'm trapped in the fire, but can't feel the rain.
I severed the ties, thought I'd feel free,
Now the silence is echoin', suffocatin' me.

I needed to break, had to cut them away,
But the fear of being lost still haunts me today.
I burn the bridges, watch the smoke rise,
But I'm left in the ruins, searchin' for the skies.

It's hard to be strong when you're standin' alone,
Burned all the bridges, but now I'm on my own.
I'll take the fall, I'll take the flame,
But the fear of isolation's still playin' the game.

Maybe I'll rise, maybe I'll fall,
But I won't stay chained, I'll risk it all.
I burned the bridges, now there's no return,
But the fire's inside, and it's startin' to burn.

Tension Between the Lines

We're speakin' in circles, but the words are thin,
  The silence is loud, and it's draggin' me in.
  Every conversation's like a war we fight,
  The tension between the lines, it's just not right.

You say you're fine, but I see the cracks,
  It's like a hidden storm that's keepin' us back.
  We dance around the truth, but it's clear as day,
  The unspoken frustration's never far away.

We're holdin' it together, but the threads are frayed,
  Like a house of cards that's startin' to sway.
  I try to reach out, but you turn away,
  The tension's buildin' up, and it's here to stay.

The words are empty, but the anger's real,
  It's a pressure cooker that we both feel.
  You say one thing, but it's never what's meant,
  The space between us is where the frustration's spent.

We're caught in this game, playin' roles so well,
  But underneath it all, we're trapped in a shell.

The silence is deafening, the gaps so wide,
The tension's pullin' us, like a dangerous tide.

I'm readin' between the lines, tryin' to see,
The cracks in the surface where we used to be.
We're walkin' on ice, afraid to break through,
The tension's a riddle we can't undo.

Every look, every word, it's a twisted game,
The unspoken fears, they're ignitin' the flame.
I want to break free, but you're holdin' tight,
The tension between us is cloudin' the light.

We're speakin' in riddles, and the lines are blurred,
The frustrations boil, but they're never heard.
We're stuck in a loop, can't find a way,
The tension's a ghost that's here to stay.

Maybe one day we'll find a way to mend,
But for now, we're trapped in this silence we defend.
The tension between the lines is a heavy weight,
And we're lost in the struggle, just tryin' to relate.

Cracks in the Facade

I'm wearin' a mask, but the cracks are showin',
  Pressure's risin', and the seams are blowin'.
  Built this facade, made it look so tight,
  But now it's splinterin' under the weight of the night.

Got the smile on lock, but it's startin' to fade,
  Every day's a battle, every moment's a charade.
  I'm holdin' it up, but the cracks start to spread,
  The perfect image I built is tearin' instead.

Underneath the surface, it's all fallin' apart,
  The cracks are wide open, revealin' my heart.
  I try to patch it up, cover the flaws,
  But the pressure's relentless, breakin' the laws.

I'm stuck in this cage, where the cracks are deep,
  Tryna keep it together, but I'm losing sleep.
  The weight of perfection is crushin' my soul,
  Every flaw that's exposed is takin' its toll.

I built this front, like I'm untouchable, strong,
  But the cracks in the facade keep draggin' me along.

The facade's crumblin', can't hold up the lies,
Every piece that falls shows the truth in disguise.

The cracks are showin', can't keep up the act,
The weight's too much, can't cover up the fact.
I'm breakin' down, the façade's givin' way,
And I'm standin' here, exposed in the fray.

Every lie, every mask, it's startin' to show,
The cracks in the facade, they're starting to grow.
I'm tryin' to keep it together, tryin' to stay sane,
But the pressure's relentless, and it's drivin' me insane.

I'm trapped in the cracks, can't fix what's undone,
The facade is breakin', and the truth has begun.
I'm layin' it bare, can't hide from the pain,
The cracks in the facade are my only refrain.

Maybe someday I'll rebuild from the wreck,
But for now, the cracks are a constant threat.
The facade's crumblin', can't keep up the pretense,
And I'm left with the truth, stripped of all pretense.

Voices in the Distance

I hear the whispers, but they're far away,
    Voices in the distance, they haunt me every day.
    Tellin' me I'm not enough, that I'll never break free,
    Every shadow's got a voice that's callin' to me.

I try to drown 'em out, turn up the sound,
    But the voices cut through, drag me to the ground.
    They say, "You're a failure, you'll never succeed,"
    Feedin' my doubts, plantin' the seed.

I'm fightin' the noise, but it's inside my head,
    Every word's a dagger, every thought's a thread.
    "Why even try? You're just wastin' your time,"
    The voices keep chippin', and I'm losin' my climb.

They mock every step, every move that I make,
    Tellin' me I'm broken, tellin' me to forsake.
    I'm stuck in this battle, can't silence the roar,
    The voices in the distance are knockin' at my door.

I tell myself I'm strong, I tell myself I'm right,
    But the voices creep closer, cuttin' through the night.

"Who do you think you are? You'll never be enough,"
The self-criticism's ruthless, it's cold and it's tough.

I try to fight back, but it's a losing game,
　　The voices in the distance keep ignitin' the flame.
　　They twist every word, they spin every lie,
　　And I'm trapped in the echoes, can't reach for the sky.

I'm drownin' in doubt, in this storm I've made,
　　The voices are relentless, they never fade.
　　"Give up now, let the darkness win,"
　　But I'm fightin' the voices that crawl under my skin.

Maybe someday I'll silence the screams,
　　But for now, I'm caught in the nightmare of dreams.
　　Voices in the distance, they won't let me be,
　　In this dialogue with doubt, I'm searchin' to be free.

Fade into Nothing

I'm driftin' away, can't find where I've been,
  Lost in the noise, where do I begin?
  The world's a cyclone, it's spinnin' me out,
  Tryna find myself, but I'm swallowed by doubt.

I'm a ghost in the crowd, just another face,
  Feelin' insignificant, like I'm outta place.
  Every day's a blur, every night's the same,
  In this chaotic world, I'm lost in the game.

I reach out for somethin', but it slips through my grasp,
  Tryna hold on, but the moments don't last.
  The chaos surrounds me, it's pullin' me down,
  I'm faded and blurred, just a shadow in town.

I scream but the sound gets swallowed by the noise,
  In this endless madness, I've lost my voice.
  Tryna stand out, but I'm drownin' in gray,
  I'm faded and lost, driftin' away.

The world's too loud, can't hear my own call,
  Feelin' so small, like I'm about to fall.

In the whirlwind of life, I'm just a breeze,
Tryna find my place, but I'm lost in the seas.

Every step feels heavy, every breath feels thin,
In this chaotic mess, where do I begin?
I'm fading into nothing, just a speck in the storm,
Lost in the chaos, where I can't transform.

I thought I'd be seen, thought I'd break through,
But the chaos consumes, and I'm stuck in the blue.
I'm a flicker of light in a world so stark,
Fadin' into nothing, lost in the dark.

Maybe someday I'll find a place to be,
But right now, I'm just lost, can't seem to break free.
In this chaotic world, where I'm feelin' so small,
I'm fading into nothing, just a shadow, that's all.

Fractured Reflections

Staring in the mirror, but I don't recognize,
　The face lookin' back, got a thousand lies.
　Shattered glass, pieces cuttin' through,
　Every crack's a wound, every edge a view.

The pain distorts what I thought was real,
　Every shard's a scar, and it's all I feel.
　I see the broken parts, can't piece 'em together,
　In this fractured reflection, I'm lost forever.

I try to smile, but it's a twisted grin,
　The pain's too deep, can't mask the sin.
　Every time I look, it's like I'm seein' through,
　A fractured image, distorted and skewed.

They say I'm fine, but they don't know the game,
　The pain's a shadow, it's burnin' my name.
　I'm trapped in the glass, can't find a way out,
　The fractured reflections, filled with doubt.

Each piece of the mirror shows a different face,
　All the broken parts, can't find my place.

I'm a collage of pain, a puzzle incomplete,
Tryna make sense of this mess at my feet.

The cracks are deep, they cut to the core,
Every reflection's a battle, a never-ending war.
I see the hurt, I see the shame,
In this fractured reflection, I'm not the same.

I reach out to mend, but the pieces won't fit,
The pain's a storm, and I'm stuck in it.
I'm lost in the shards, can't see the whole,
Fractured reflections, shatterin' my soul.

Maybe one day I'll find a way to heal,
But for now, I'm trapped in this fractured reel.
In the mirror's shattered view, I'm searchin' for light,
But the reflections are broken, and I'm lost in the night.

Scars Left Behind

I wear the scars like a badge of disgrace,
Each one a story, etched on my face.
Betrayal's the ink, disappointment's the knife,
Cut so deep, it's a part of my life.

Every mark's a memory, a wound that won't heal,
The scars left behind are the pain I feel.
Trust was a game, but I lost every round,
The cuts in my soul are the pain I found.

I try to forget, but the scars don't fade,
Each one's a reminder of the choices I made.
Every scar's a lesson, a bitter regret,
In the gallery of pain, my heart's a set.

I trusted too much, thought I had it all,
But betrayal's a crash, and I took the fall.
The scars are the echoes of the trust that was broken,
The silence of lies, the pain unspoken.

These scars are my armor, my shield in the fight,
But they're also the burden I carry each night.

I wear them with pride, but they're heavy to bear,
A constant reminder of the hurt that's still there.

I'm haunted by shadows, by the scars left behind,
In the battlefield of trust, I'm scarred and confined.
Each mark's a story, each cut's a chapter,
In the book of betrayal, the pain's the master.

I try to heal, but the wounds still sting,
The scars left behind are a painful ring.
I'll wear them with honor, though they cut me deep,
In the journey of life, these scars I'll keep.

Maybe someday I'll find a way to mend,
But for now, the scars are my only friend.
In the mirror's reflection, they're the truth I find,
The scars left behind, the pain intertwined.

Into the Static

I'm drownin' in the noise, can't hear my own thoughts,
   The static's overload, and I'm lost in the knots.
   Tryna break through the chaos, but it's all in my head,
   The mental noise is a storm, got me seein' red.

Every thought's a static, a jumbled mess,
   I'm lost in the signal, can't escape the stress.
   I scream for clarity, but the echoes don't fade,
   Caught in the static, feelin' trapped and betrayed.

The white noise is deafening, it's all that I know,
   Tryna cut through the haze, but I'm stuck in the flow.
   The static's a barrier, a wall that I can't climb,
   Every step I take, I'm fallin' behind.

I'm searchin' for the signal, a spark in the dark,
   But the static's relentless, it's leavin' its mark.
   My mind's a battlefield, the noise is the war,
   Tryna find a way out, but I'm stuck at the core.

The static's a veil, it's coverin' my sight,
   Lost in the confusion, can't find the light.

Every whisper's distorted, every thought's a haze,
In this mental fog, I'm trapped in a maze.

I'm fightin' the static, tryin' to clear the air,
But the noise is a prison, and it's makin' me swear.
I'm drownin' in the chaos, tryin' to stay sane,
But the static's a monster, and it's drivin' me insane.

Maybe someday I'll find a way to break free,
But for now, I'm lost in the noise inside of me.
Into the static, where my thoughts intertwine,
Caught in the confusion, tryna redefine.

Behind Closed Doors

You see the smile, but you don't see the cracks,
Behind closed doors, where the darkness attacks.
Got a public face, but it's all just a mask,
The real struggle's hidden, but who's gonna ask?

I play the part, put on the perfect show,
But behind the curtains, it's a different glow.
The battle's inside, where the demons creep,
In the shadows of my room, where I lie awake, deep.

The world sees the picture, the image so clean,
But the truth is a monster, and it's never been seen.
I'm fightin' my wars, where no one can see,
Behind closed doors, that's where I'm just me.

Every smile's a lie, every laugh's a disguise,
The pain's in the silence, where the truth never lies.
I hide behind the jokes, the stories I tell,
But behind closed doors, it's a personal hell.

I'm trapped in the echo, the sound of my fears,
The struggle's a whisper, it's been hidin' for years.

I build up the walls, keep the pain out of sight,
But behind closed doors, it's a long, lonely fight.

You think you know me, but you see just a show,
The real battles are fought where the light doesn't go.
I wear the facade, but it's crackin' and thin,
Behind closed doors, where my true fight begins.

Every tear's a secret, every cry's a plea,
In the quiet of my room, that's where I'm truly me.
The world gets the mask, the polished display,
But behind closed doors, I'm lost in the gray.

I'm holdin' it together, but it's breakin' me down,
Behind closed doors, I'm wearin' a frown.
Maybe someday the truth will break through the seams,
But for now, I'm hidin' behind the scenes.

Stumbling Through the Noise

I'm lost in the chaos, can't hear my own voice,
The world's a loud mess, and I'm makin' no choice.
Stumbling through the noise, it's a brutal game,
Tryna find some clarity, but it's all just the same.

Every sound's a hammer, beatin' on my brain,
The chaos is a beast, and it's drivin' me insane.
I'm drownin' in the clamor, can't catch a breath,
In this whirlwind of chaos, I'm close to the edge.

The world's a storm, and I'm caught in the rain,
Every drop's a distraction, every splash is pain.
Tryna find a path, but the noise's too loud,
I'm lost in the crowd, can't see through the shroud.

I'm reachin' for silence, but it's out of my grasp,
In the middle of the storm, I'm gaspin' for a gasp.
The chaos is relentless, it's a tidal wave,
Tryna swim through the noise, but I'm feelin' so enslaved.

Every word's a blur, every sound's a mess,
I'm searchin' for the calm, but I'm stuck in distress.

The noise is a prison, and I'm fightin' to break,
Tryna find a moment where I can finally awake.

I stumble through the static, tryna catch a break,
But the chaos keeps comin', with every step I take.
The world's in a frenzy, and I'm lost in the fray,
Tryna find some clarity, but it's slippin' away.

I'm trapped in the noise, can't hear my own mind,
In this battlefield of sound, I'm tryin' to find.
Maybe someday I'll break through, find some peace,
But for now, I'm stumbling, lookin' for release.

Weight of the Moment

The weight of the moment, it's crushin' my chest,
    Every emotion's a storm, no room for rest.
    It hits like a freight train, all at once,
    Got me pinned down, can't even confront.

Heart's racin', mind's in a mess,
    Drowning in the feelings, can't seem to suppress.
    The moment's a beast, and it's takin' its toll,
    Every wave crashes, swallowin' me whole.

I'm gaspin' for air, but the pressure's too thick,
    The emotions collide, it's a brutal mix.
    No space to breathe, no chance to clear,
    In the weight of the moment, I'm trapped in fear.

Each feeling's a hammer, poundin' on my soul,
    The intensity's relentless, it's outta control.
    I try to hold on, but it's breakin' me down,
    In this flood of emotions, I'm startin' to drown.

The moment's a monster, it's steal'n my breath,
    Every burst of emotion feels like a death.

I'm fightin' the weight, tryin' to stay afloat,
But the flood keeps comin', and it's draggin' my boat.

Every second's a struggle, every beat's a fight,
The weight of the moment's crushin' my light.
I'm lost in the chaos, can't find a way out,
Drowning in the weight, can't scream, can't shout.

Maybe someday I'll find a way to cope,
But for now, I'm buried in the moment's rope.
It's an avalanche of feelings, no room to breathe,
In the weight of the moment, I'm left to seethe.

Distant Horizons

I'm starin' at the horizon, but it's too far to see,
The future's callin' me, but it's chained to uncertainty.
I'm reachin' for change, but it's slippin' away,
Like a shadow in the distance, I'm stuck in the gray.

The road ahead's blurry, the path's unclear,
But the need to move forward's burnin' fierce in here.
I'm caught in the middle, between fear and desire,
Yearnin' for somethin', but I'm stuck in the fire.

Every step I take feels like a fall,
The horizon's callin', but I'm scared of it all.
The unknown's a monster, it's pullin' me back,
But I'm tired of the same, I'm tired of the lack.

I want to break free, but I'm scared to let go,
The distant horizons, they're startin' to glow.
But the light's too bright, and the dark's too deep,
Caught in the middle where my doubts still creep.

I'm runnin' in place, but my heart's still torn,
Between the life I've known and the dreams I've worn.

I can taste the change, but it's just outta reach,
And the fear of the unknown's got me stuck on repeat.

The horizon's a promise, but it's also a threat,
I'm drawn to the future, but I'm filled with regret.
I want to take the leap, but I'm scared of the fall,
So I stand on the edge, doin' nothin' at all.

Maybe someday I'll gather the strength,
To run toward the future, to close the length.
But for now, I'm stuck, caught in the grind,
Yearnin' for those distant horizons I'll someday find.

Whispers of Control

You speak so soft, but the message is clear,
  Whispers of control, draggin' me near.
  Pullin' the strings like I'm your puppet to play,
  I can feel your grip, but I can't break away.

Every word's a lie wrapped in disguise,
  I can see the truth burnin' behind your eyes.
  You smile, you laugh, but I know what's real,
  The way you twist my mind just to make me feel.

Like I owe you somethin', like I can't stand tall,
  Whispers in my ear, you're buildin' the wall.
  Every promise you make is just another chain,
  Holdin' me down while I suffocate in pain.

You pull me in close, then push me away,
  Like a game you play, leavin' me in dismay.
  I try to stand up, but you're quick with the grip,
  Manipulation masked in your voice, slick with the flip.

Every move I make, you're there in the shadows,
  Tuggin' on the strings, I'm trapped in your gallows.

You make me doubt myself, you make me weak,
In the whispers of control, I can't even speak.

I'm fightin' to break free, but the ties are tight,
You're craftin' my world, takin' away my fight.
The whispers are louder now, echoes in my head,
I'm a pawn in your game, where the truth's been dead.

But I see through the lies, and I'm findin' my voice,
Won't be trapped anymore, won't be your choice.
The whispers are fadin', your control's fallin' apart,
I'm breakin' the strings, reclaimin' my heart.

You can whisper your lies, but I won't bend,
I'm stronger now—this is where it ends.

Fragmented Pieces

I'm shattered, broken, feelin' like a mess,
　　Fragmented pieces of my soul, can't confess.
　　Every thought's scattered, every breath's tight,
　　Tryna hold it together, but I'm losin' the fight.

I look in the mirror, don't know who I see,
　　The cracks in my mind keep tearin' at me.
　　The weight's gettin' heavy, can't bear the load,
　　Each piece of me fallin', nowhere to go.

It's like I'm split in two, can't find my place,
　　Fragmented pieces, lost in space.
　　I smile on the outside, but inside I break,
　　Everything's fallin' and it's more than I can take.

The voices keep screamin', echo in my head,
　　Tellin' me I'm nothin', pushin' me to the edge.
　　I'm losin' control, can't find my ground,
　　The cracks are spreadin', no way to come around.

I try to stay strong, but I'm slippin' fast,
　　The pieces of me fallin', no way they'll last.

Each day's a battle, every step's a crawl,
I'm losin' my grip, and I'm ready to fall.

It's a puzzle I can't solve, no pieces that fit,
Fragmented pieces, breakin' bit by bit.
No way to repair, no way to rewind,
Just livin' in fragments, tryna find some peace of mind.

I'm fightin' the fall, but I'm tired, I'm spent,
The pieces of me gone, can't figure where they went.
I'm torn in the middle, stuck in the cracks,
Fragmented pieces, no way to come back.

Maybe one day I'll find a way to mend,
But right now I'm broken, can't pretend.
Fragmented pieces, fallin' to the floor,
I'm pickin' 'em up, but I'm breakin' more.

Buried Screams

I'm screamin' inside, but no one can hear,
Buried beneath all the doubt and the fear.
Every word's trapped, can't break the seal,
Feelin' so heavy, but can't let it spill.

I try to speak out, but the silence is loud,
The weight of my pain got me lost in the crowd.
Nobody's listenin', they just turn away,
While I'm suffocatin', day after day.

I'm drownin' in thoughts that I can't let loose,
Like a noose 'round my neck, there's no excuse.
Feelin' the pressure, I'm ready to break,
But no one's around to feel what's at stake.

Buried screams, locked in my chest,
I hold it all in, can't put it to rest.
Every shout's muffled, every tear's fake,
I'm trapped in my head, how much more can I take?

You see me smilin', but it's all a disguise,
Behind these eyes, there's a storm that's on the rise.

I wanna let go, I wanna explode,
But the screams stay buried, deep in my soul.

It's like I'm stuck in a cage with no key,
All this rage and hurt, eatin' at me.
Nobody asks, nobody cares,
I'm dyin' inside, but nobody's there.

So I bite my tongue, let the silence win,
Holdin' it all in, beneath my skin.
Every day's a fight, but no one sees,
The buried screams echoin' in the breeze.

Maybe one day, I'll find a way to shout,
To break through the silence, to let it all out.
But for now, I'm stuck, chained to this dream,
Of a voice that's lost in buried screams.

Beneath the Ashes

Beneath the ashes, I'm tryin' to rise,
    Burned to the core, but I'm still alive.
    Everything crumbled, went up in flames,
    But I'm clawing my way out, not playin' your games.

The fire left scars, but I'm not done,
    Tryna rebuild from what's been undone.
    The smoke still lingers, the pain's still real,
    But beneath the ashes, I'm startin' to heal.

You tried to break me, left me in the dirt,
    Thought I'd stay buried, crushed by the hurt.
    But now I'm standin', from ruin I climb,
    Risin' from the wreckage, takin' back what's mine.

Every tear, every scar, every broken dream,
    Beneath the ashes, I'm stronger than I seem.
    I was lost in the flames, couldn't find my way,
    But I'm pullin' myself out, day by day.

The past keeps hauntin', the memories sting,
    But I won't let the burn take everything.

I'm fightin' the shadows, pushin' through the smoke,
The weight of destruction, but I refuse to choke.

You thought I was done, thought I'd disappear,
But beneath the ashes, I'm still right here.
Piece by piece, I'm rebuildin' my soul,
Risin' from nothin', takin' back control.

Every step's heavy, every breath's tough,
But I'm pushin' through when it's never enough.
I'm standin' tall now, though the pain's still near,
Beneath the ashes, I've conquered the fear.

From the rubble, I'm buildin' a throne,
This is my rise, I'm takin' it home.
You can't break me, I'm claimin' my name,
Beneath the ashes, I've risen from the flame.

Beneath the Surface

Beneath the surface, it's all breakin' apart,
   Keepin' it cool, but I'm losin' heart.
   You see the smile, but you don't know the storm,
   Inside I'm burnin', outside I'm warm.

I'm holdin' it down while I'm fallin' to pieces,
   Feelin' the pressure, and nobody sees this.
   The cracks in my mind that I can't show,
   Beneath the surface, I'm ready to blow.

I wear this mask so you don't ask,
   Keepin' it quiet, it's my only task.
   But under the calm, there's chaos at play,
   I'm fightin' the breakdown every single day.

My thoughts are racin', I can't slow 'em down,
   Drownin' in silence, but I won't let it drown.
   You think I'm steady, like I'm in control,
   But beneath the surface, I'm losin' my soul.

I'm trapped in my head, but you'll never know,
   Wearin' this calm while I'm ready to blow.

Every word I speak feels empty, fake,
Beneath the surface, I'm ready to break.

I keep it together, I hide the mess,
But inside I'm crumblin', filled with distress.
The weight of it all, the cracks in disguise,
Beneath the surface, I'm sinkin' in lies.

You think I'm okay, but I'm barely afloat,
Caught in this battle, stuck in my throat.
The calm you see? It's just a façade,
Beneath the surface, I'm lost in the fog.

One day it'll break, one day it'll show,
And all this pressure will finally blow.
But 'til that moment, I keep it concealed,
Beneath the surface, I'm beggin' to heal.

Breathing through the Breaks

I'm holdin' on, breathin' through the breaks,
  Life's crashin' down, I'm feelin' the shakes.
  Every step's harder, every move's slow,
  But I keep pushin' 'cause I can't let go.

I'm standin' in the wreckage, caught in the storm,
  Feelin' like I'm shattered, can't find the norm.
  But I take a breath, let it fill my chest,
  Keep my head high, even when I'm stressed.

The cracks are showin', I'm fallin' apart,
  But I won't let it break me, I'm protectin' my heart.
  Every day's a struggle, but I'm still in the game,
  Breathin' through the breaks, tryin' to stay sane.

It's like I'm climbin', but the ground's givin' way,
  Feelin' like I'm losin', but I'm here to stay.
  Every tear I hide, every shout I bury,
  Breathin' through the breaks when it's gettin' scary.

You can see the strain, but you don't see the fight,
  Holdin' it together in the dead of the night.

I'm torn at the seams, but I won't quit,
Breathin' through the breaks, I'm dealin' with it.

The pressure's risin', I feel it inside,
But I keep my cool, won't let it collide.
Every breath I take, I'm holdin' the weight,
Breathin' through the breaks before it's too late.

I know I'm fallin', but I'm learnin' to fly,
Through the breaks and the cracks, I'm touchin' the sky.
The pieces are scattered, but I'm still here,
Breathin' through the breaks, fightin' the fear.

Even when it feels like I'm about to break down,
I take a breath and stand my ground.
I'm stronger than the fractures, stronger than the fall,
Breathin' through the breaks—I can face it all.

Lines We've Crossed

I've crossed lines that I can't step back,
    Fought too hard, now it's all turned black.
    Screamin' for someone to hear my voice,
    But in the silence, I lost the choice.

Pushed too far just to make 'em see,
    Now I'm trapped in the mess of who I used to be.
    Every word I've thrown, every fight I've sparked,
    Left me standing here, alone in the dark.

I tried so hard, but the walls won't break,
    The deeper I go, the more I take.
    Runnin' on fumes, but I can't turn 'round,
    Crossed too many lines, now I'm lost in the sound.

The louder I shout, the more I fade,
    Caught in the noise of the mess I've made.
    Wanted to be heard, but they just shut me down,
    Now I'm drownin' in the lines that I've crossed in this town.

Every step's been a battle, every breath's a fight,
    And I can't see the way out, trapped in the night.

All these lines I've crossed, just tryin' to be seen,
But I'm stuck in a nightmare, far from the dream.

The scars on my soul, the fire in my chest,
I keep pushin' forward, but I'm never at rest.
The more that I scream, the less that they care,
Crossed too many lines, now I'm gaspin' for air.

I burned the bridges, cut the ties,
Now I'm buried in the things I can't disguise.
Pushed past the point where the damage is done,
And the lines I've crossed, they can't be undone.

I wanted to matter, I wanted to break free,
But now I'm just a shadow of who I used to be.
Crossed too many lines, now I'm payin' the cost,
Tryin' to find myself in everything I've lost.

After the Fall

After the fall, I'm stuck in the dirt,
    Pickin' up pieces, still feelin' the hurt.
    The wreckage around me, it's all I can see,
    But somehow I'm pushin', still tryin' to be me.

I hit rock bottom, thought I'd never rise,
    But I'm diggin' through the rubble, fightin' the lies.
    The scars still burn, the pain still stays,
    But I'm standin' tall, findin' my way.

I'm bruised, I'm broken, but I'm not done,
    After the fall, I'm still holdin' on.
    Every step forward, it feels like a fight,
    But I'll keep pushin' through, even in the night.

The ground gave way, and I hit hard,
    But I'm pullin' myself up, inch by inch, scar by scar.
    Every tear, every loss, it's part of the climb,
    After the fall, I'll rise in my own time.

They thought I was finished, left me to break,
    But they don't know the fire, the will I'll take.

I'm piecin' it together, buildin' it strong,
After the fall, I'm provin' 'em wrong.

The echoes of failure still haunt my mind,
But in the ruins, a strength I find.
The pieces are jagged, but they'll fit somehow,
After the fall, I'm here, I'm now.

I've been through the worst, I've felt it all,
But I'm standin' tall after the fall.
Rebuildin' the life that I thought was gone,
After the fall, I'll keep movin' on.

Through the dust, through the pain, I'll reclaim my name,
After the fall, I'll never be the same.
But stronger, bolder, I'm fightin' my call,
After the fall, I'll rise above it all.

Silenced Shouts

I'm screamin' inside but nobody hears,
My words get drowned in a sea of fears.
Silenced shouts, trapped in my chest,
Feelin' the weight, but I can't express.

I'm yellin' for help, but it's fallin' on stone,
Feels like I'm talkin', but I'm still alone.
These thoughts are loud, they echo in my mind,
But every time I speak, I get left behind.

I've got all these words but no one to say 'em to,
My voice goes quiet, but the pain shines through.
I'm fightin' for a way to break out of this sound,
But every time I try, I just get shut down.

I'm punchin' the walls, but they don't crack,
No one can hear the screams holdin' me back.
They look at me like I'm fine, like I'm whole,
But inside, I'm losin' control.

These silenced shouts are too much to bear,
But no one's listenin', no one's there.

I'm breakin' down, but it's all in my head,
And on the outside, they think I'm just dead.

I scream in the mirror, but it won't scream back,
My voice fades out while the pressure stacks.
I'm fightin' for a place where I can be real,
But my silenced shouts, they're all I feel.

I'm tearin' apart, I'm fallin' in place,
And every shout leaves a deeper trace.
But still, I'm trapped, no one around,
My shouts are silent, but I'm screamin' loud.

Faint Footsteps

I'm walkin' through shadows, can't find the light,
    Every step's a battle, every night's a fight.
    Faint footsteps echo in the void,
    Keep movin' forward, though I'm paranoid.

I'm out in the dark, where the world can't see,
    But I'm pushin' on, tryna set myself free.
    Each step is heavy, but I make it count,
    Even when I'm drowned in a silence that mounts.

No one notices, no one hears my strain,
    But I keep goin', walkin' through the pain.
    These faint footsteps are all I've got,
    Keepin' me goin' when I'm feelin' forgot.

I'm tryin' to make waves, but the tides won't turn,
    Feelin' invisible, but I still yearn.
    Every step's a whisper in the deafening roar,
    But I keep movin' forward, lookin' for more.

No cheers, no claps, just the sound of my feet,
    Trudgin' through the dark, but I won't admit defeat.

Faint footsteps, but they're steady and true,
Pushing through the silence, fightin' for my view.

I'm drownin' in the noise, but I hold my pace,
Every step's a victory in this endless race.
Even when I'm lost, and the path's unclear,
I'm movin' forward, despite the fear.

So I keep on walkin', though the world's gone cold,
Faint footsteps in the dark, but my story's still told.
Invisible to many, but I'm fightin' my fight,
Every faint step brings me closer to the light.

In the Eye of the Storm

Caught in the cyclone, spinnin' outta control,
   Heart's in a frenzy, but I'm holdin' my soul.
   In the eye of the storm, where it's calm but frail,
   I find a moment's peace before the next gale.

The wind's roarin' loud, the chaos surrounds,
   But in this small circle, I hear no sounds.
   It's quiet, it's still, like a temporary peace,
   A brief respite where my worries cease.

I'm watchin' the storm rage, feelin' its might,
   But in the center, I'm lost in the night.
   This calm is an illusion, a fleeting disguise,
   A brief, fragile break 'fore the storm's next rise.

I'm breathin' in slowly, savin' my grace,
   In the eye of the storm, in this fleeting space.
   I know it won't last, this calm won't stay,
   But I'm takin' the silence while it's here, okay?

The storm's just a tempest, the chaos is real,
   But in this moment, I'm startin' to heal.

It's a calm in the chaos, a pause in the fight,
A brief moment of clarity in the dead of the night.

The storm's gonna hit, the winds will howl,
But I'll take this calm, let it teach me how.
To find a brief peace in the middle of strife,
Even if it's fleeting, it's part of my life.

So I stand in the eye, feel the stillness collide,
With the raging storm on the other side.
It's a temporary calm, but I'll take what I can,
In the eye of the storm, I'll make my stand.

Breathe Again

I'm crawlin' out of the wreckage, dust in my lungs,
  Strugglin' to rise, but the pain still stings.
  Every breath's a battle, every moment's a strain,
  But I'm fightin' through the chaos, breakin' these chains.

I've been at the edge, where the darkness falls,
  But now I'm seein' light through these shattered walls.
  I'm takin' it slow, but I'm startin' to mend,
  Breathin' in deep, findin' strength to ascend.

I used to be shattered, fragments on the floor,
  But I'm piecin' it together, finding more than before.
  The scars are still there, but they're part of my skin,
  And I'm learnin' to breathe again, let the healing begin.

Every breath is a victory, a step toward the sky,
  Clawin' out of the darkness, where the shadows lie.
  It's a slow, steady climb, but I'm reachin' the top,
  Breathin' in the future, letting the past drop.

I'm feelin' the pulse of life in my veins,
  Findin' the rhythm in the midst of the pains.

I'm startin' to smile where the tears used to fall,
Breathin' again, standin' tall through it all.

The weight's still heavy, but I'm pushin' through,
Learning to breathe, findin' strength anew.
The fight's not over, but I'm feelin' alive,
Breathin' again, and I'm startin' to thrive.

Every breath is a testament to the battles I've faced,
Each one a reminder that I'm not erased.
I'm takin' the pain and I'm makin' it mine,
Breathin' again, and I'm takin' back time.

So here I am, rising from the ashes again,
Breathin' in the freedom, letting go of the end.
Finding my rhythm, where the chaos has been,
Breathin' again, startin' over again.

www.ingramcontent.com/pod-product-compliance
Lightning Source LLC
Chambersburg PA
CBHW052226150726
48002CB00003B/1302